NATURE'S \

MW01168494

Edited by Nicole Carmichael

Written by James Marsh

WORLD BOOK / TWO-CAN

NATURE'S WILD

First published in the United States in 1996
by World Book Inc.
525 W. Monroe
20th Floor
Chicago
IL USA 60661
in association with Two-Can Publishing Ltd.

Copyright © Two-Can Publishing Ltd 1996

**For information on other World Book products,
call 1-800-255-1750, x 2238.**

ISBN 0-7166-1736-6 (pbk.)
LC: 96-60465

Printed in Hong Kong

1 2 3 4 5 6 7 8 9 10 99 98 97 96

All rights reserved. No part of this publication may be reproduced,
stored in a retrieval system or transmitted in any form or by any
means electronic, mechanical, photocopying, recording or
otherwise, without prior written permission of the publisher.

Design by Simon Relph. Picture research by Debbie Dorman. Production by Joya Bart-Plange.

Front cover photograph: Bruce Coleman Ltd. Inserts: Bruce Coleman Ltd.: l&c. Oxford Scientific Films: r.

Picture credits: Oxford Scientific Films: 4l, 5bl&tr, 6r, 10bl&tc, 11l, 12b, 12/13c, 13tr, 15tr, 17tl,tr&br, 18bc, 18/19, 24c, 26tl, 27c, 28t, 29b, 30tl, 31br.
Bruce Coleman Ltd.: 4r, 5tl, 6/7, 7tl, 9 br, 12/13b, 14, 14/15t&b, 15 br, 19 tl&c, 20r, 21bl, 22, 22/23, 22tr&br&trc, 24tc&br, 25bc, 26/27, 27br, 28c, 29t,
30r, 31tc. Heather Angel/Biofotos: 4c, 10tl&bc, 16tr, 17br, 18tl, 21br, 23tc, 30bl, 31tl&bl. WWF(UK): 8r. Nature Photographers: 8/9t, 9tr,
A-Z Botanical: 8/9b, p20tl, 21tc, 23cr, 25tl&br, 26c, 27 tr. PA News: 10cr. Mary Evans: 19bc.

Illustrations: Chris West: 11. Woody: 13, 19.

CONTENTS

THEY'RE OL

The plant kingdom is millions of years old, but it's still growing strong!

And plants still have relatives alive today.

By the time that dinosaurs were roaming the world, great forests had become established. But the leaves and branches that plant-eating dinosaurs munched on looked very different from today's greenery. For example, hardly anything grew flowers – flowering plants weren't common until around 80 million years ago!

Fossilized fern leaves (above), petrified wood (right), and birds'-nest ferns (left), descendants of a bygone age

Around a billion years ago, long before the reign of the mighty dinosaurs, plants began to evolve. But it wasn't until around 360,000,000 B.C. that major land plants appeared. Then, about 115 million years later, cycads and ferns began to flourish,

TREEMENDOUS!
Most ancient plants are now extinct, and what we know about them has been discovered by examining remains. Whole trees were turned into fossils in North America's petrified forests,

DER THAN DINOSAURS!

▲ *The amazing ancient ginkgo from China*

some with trunks 100 feet long. However, there is a species of tree dating back to the days of the dinosaur that still survives today.

The ginkgo, or maidenhair, tree is a living fossil that first appeared about 180 million years ago. Other species of a mere 100 million years ago also survive, but the ginkgo is our only living link to the age of the dinosaur.

The world's oldest living thing is thought to be a 10,000-year-old lichen from Antarctica. Cool!

ROOTS IN HISTORY

To ensure their species' survival, plants try to spread their seeds far and wide. To do this, they use all sorts of tricks. One clever type of grass began to produce a seed 10,000 years ago that a particular animal liked to eat. The animal encouraged the seed to grow by transporting it farther afield, and that grass can now be found in vast areas all over the world. The name of the animal? Man. And the name of the grass? Wheat.

In a similar way, many plants have seeds called burrs that hook themselves to animal fur. The animal picks off the seeds later, leaving

▲ *The most successful plant in the world, wheat*

▲ *One of the oldest trees on the planet, the mighty bristlecone pine*

them to grow in a different place from where they started. Meanwhile, other plants are spreading their seeds far and wide, riding on the wind.

HAPPY BIRTHDAY

Clocking up an impressive 4,700 years, a bristlecone pine tree in the White Mountains of California is the oldest known living tree on the planet. Another pine from the same group died there recently — at the grand old age of 5,100 years old! What's more, it's thought that some of the pines there

will live to be 5,500!

Most plants are unlikely to live one-hundredth of the time that a bristlecone pine is expected to survive, but each and every plant has a life packed full of surprises.

From trees that grow bigger than anything else on the planet, to deadly varieties that poison with just one leaf, nature really is wild.

But be warned, plants are so fascinating they're bound to grow on you!

Unlike animals, which need all sorts of elements to survive, all that plants need is water, warmth, light, and some nutrients. They have the ability to use water and light as well as carbon dioxide from the air to actually make food for themselves.

What's even more amazing is that through this process (called photosynthesis) oxygen is produced. Without plants, we wouldn't be able to breathe.

In deserts, on mountains, and at the polar ice caps, plants' essential ingredients of survival can be difficult to find. So those that do find water, light, etc., are some of the hardiest members of the plant world.

SHARP PRACTICE

In deserts, water is always scarce. Plants have few leaves, and many keep their water reserves hidden in swollen buds underground. The odd-looking welwitschia of Africa has just two leaves, although they can be up to 60 feet long. They curl around the base of the plant, collecting dew and channeling it back to the main plant and into a large under-ground root.

In North American deserts, the cactus is king – from prickly pears to the giant *Pachycereus grandi* that grows to 80 feet tall. These cacti store water inside a hard, waxy, trunk, and they're armed with sharp spines to keep thirsty animals away. When rain does come, the cacti suck up the water very quickly – the huge saguaro cactus can take in over a ton of water during a single rainstorm.

Rain, however, is very rare in a desert, so plants make the most of it, suddenly turning what seemed to be barren land into a carpet of color. One African plant, the *Boerhavia repens*, takes just eight days to grow from a seed into a mature plant. It even produces seeds of its own. Hot stuff!

COLD COMFORT

Conditions for plants near the polar ice caps are harsh. It's very cold, freezing winds howl across the snow, and sunlight is very weak. In fact, for six months of the year it is completely dark. But, amazingly, some survive here. Red-colored algae live in these

▶ *The gila woodpecker escapes from the desert heat by making its nest inside the massive saguaro cactus, where it can be a comfortable 50°F cooler than outside.*

▲ *Even in barren deserts, the prickly pear blossoms.*

THE SURVIVORS!

Plants shoot up even in the world's harshest environments

▲ *The Arctic poppy survives winter by soaking up summer sun.*

polar regions, waiting for the summer sun to melt the top layer of snow. As it begins to thaw, these tiny organisms make their way to the surface, turning huge areas of snow red.

The Arctic poppy is another snowy survivor. It waits until the Arctic summer arrives before flowering; then it constantly sunbathes, soaking up the heat and light before the cold winter returns.

WINTER WARMERS

High up in the mountains where the snow can stay all year round, some plants like the alpine edelweiss protect themselves from the cold by growing wooly hairs on their leaves and flowers.

The saussurea from the Himalayas has taken this furry protection one step further. It grows a blanket of fur around itself as insulation, and insects often spend the night inside the blanket to keep warm. Snug as a bug!

DOUBLE TROUBLE

Plants on Mount Kenya in Africa have twice as many problems. The mountain is on the equator, which means that during the day the sun blazes with the same power as it does in the driest deserts. At night, though, the temperature plummets, due to the height of the mountain. Water freezes, and plants that were earlier basking in the sun have to protect themselves from the teeth-chattering cold. One giant groundsel wraps its tender buds up with its hardy outside leaves. As soon as the sun comes up in the morning, the outer leaves open to allow the plant to warm itself and bask once more.

▲ *Wooly hairs keep the Alpine edelweiss warm.*

EMERGENCY!

Precious plants in danger

Plants are under threat the world over, and it's almost all because of people's activities. Large areas of tropical rain forest are constantly being destroyed to provide land for farming and housing. As well as cutting down trees, loggers are wiping out plants. And once a plant becomes extinct, it's gone forever.

▼ THE WORLD'S RAREST

Islands often have species of plants that are unique to them, and because they're

> In the United States and Mexico, rare cacti are dug up in the middle of the night and sold to the wealthy for their gardens.

on islands, many of these plants are very rare.

Rodriguez Island near Madagascar has many rare plants, but none as precious as the cafe marron. It was thought that this medicinal plant had become extinct; then in 1980 a sharp-eyed schoolboy noticed one old tree had survived. Fences were put around it to protect it, and now it has a full-time guard to keep thieves at bay.

Botanical experts from Kew Gardens in London took a cutting of the tree and were able to grow ten more. These will help to repopulate Rodriguez Island, and botanists hope there will be many more cafe marron trees for years to come.

SECRET SEEDS

Easter Island is famous for the skill of its wood-carvers, but, amazingly, there are no trees there! There used to be forests, but all of the trees were used for making canoes and houses and moving the big statues that the island is famous for. In the late 1950s, the last of the native toromiro trees was cut down for firewood, and the species was declared extinct.

Fortunately, an explorer had collected some seeds from the last tree, and he gave them to botanical centers. Using the seeds, botanists grew new trees in Europe and Chile. Now, over 100 toromiros have been replanted on Easter Island.

COLLECTOR'S CORNER

Some plants, like Chile's blue crocus (below), have become rare in the wild because they have been overcollected by gardeners. Now they can only be found in special collections. In Turkey millions of bulbs are dug up every year to sell to European garden centers, and snowdrops (right) are thought to be in particular danger.

▲ RARE PEAR

One of Britain's rarest trees is the Plymouth pear. It was first established in 1865 and used to be a common sight, with its distinctive blossom and tiny pears. Now it only exists in the wild in two places. The good news is it's now protected by law, and a plan is blossoming to get more trees on the map.

16th century, much of the forest was destroyed for farming. Then animals were introduced and proceeded to overgraze the island. Seven plant species have been wiped out, but now a conservation program has been launched to save native species such as the ebony tree. Let's hope it's not too late.

TULIP LINE

Every spring in Greece, botanists gather to marvel at the rare wild tulips. One of the rarest, Goulimy's red tulip, faces possible extinction because of farmers plowing up land. Children also dig up the precious bulbs, as they've discovered they're delicious. Find an apple instead, kids!

▶ TREASURE ISLAND

Several species of plants have been totally wiped out on the South Atlantic island of St. Helena. After people began to settle there in the

WAIT FOR IT!

Some flowers grow like wildfire, but not everything happens quickly in the plant world!

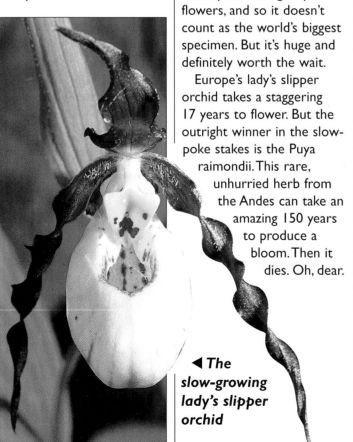

▲ *The spectacular titan arum in full bloom*

SECRET SEVEN

Most plants flower every year – or at least once every two years, but the titan arum from Sumatra waits seven years before it's ready to come into bloom. Every year it grows a tall leaf that helps the plant to store food in a huge underground bulb, or corm. But when it gets around to flowering it really flowers!

The trumpetlike bloom is nearly 3 feet wide and the spike that grows out of it can be over 8 feet tall! However, although titan arum looks like a flower, it's actually a whole group of flowers, and so it doesn't count as the world's biggest specimen. But it's huge and definitely worth the wait.

Europe's lady's slipper orchid takes a staggering 17 years to flower. But the outright winner in the slow-poke stakes is the Puya raimondii. This rare, unhurried herb from the Andes can take an amazing 150 years to produce a bloom. Then it dies. Oh, dear.

◀ *The slow-growing lady's slipper orchid*

▲ *Ancient Arctic lupins*

FREEZE FRAME

Seeds can take a few years to germinate, but the Arctic lupin holds the record for being the most patient. Some of the seeds that were found in frozen river silt in Canada were between 10,000 and 15,000 years old! When they were eventually planted, they grew amazingly well and even flowered!

▲ *The towering 150-year-old Puya raimondii*

ON A GROW SLOW

Near the North and South poles, the weather is so cold that plants can only grow two or three days a year. Some lichens growing on rocks just 300 miles from the South Pole take 60 years to grow a mere $3/8$ inch !

▲ *LIAR!*

The century plant was so named because people believed it only flowered once every 100 years. In fact, this plant that comes from Mexico usually blooms after only 10 years!

MOMENT OF GLORY

Some flowers, like those of the morning-glory family, live for just one day and then die. In that time the plant has to shed its own pollen and be fertilized by another plant's pollen. Fingers crossed!

WOW!

The most massive living thing on earth isn't a jumbo elephant or a whopping whale – it's a giant sequoia (also called redwood) tree that grows in California.

The tree is so famous it's even been given its own name, General Sherman, and it's a massive 275 feet – that's the same height as 53 adults standing on each other's shoulders!

Tree experts reckon that if General Sherman was chopped down (perish the thought!) it would weigh over 1,400 tons – that's the same weight as 360 elephants! It would also provide enough wood to make 5,000,000,000 (five billion!) matches. Strike a light!

SCALING NEW HEIGHTS

General Sherman may be a giant heavyweight, but, amazingly, it's not the tallest living tree on the planet. That title goes to another redwood in California, which is more than 366 feet high. But even that has some growing to do before it equals the world-record holder. When this particular Australian mountain ash tree was measured in 1872, it topped a whopping 433 feet, and almost certainly measured over 492 feet at its peak! And that's no tall story!

◄ *When it comes to tall trees, General Sherman tops the lot! See how it measures up against the man standing next to it!*

HIGH FLIERS

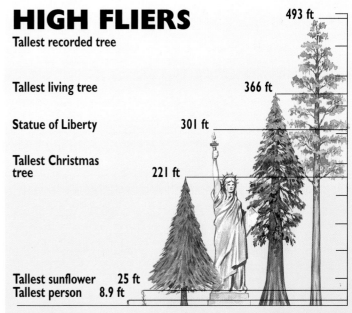

Tallest recorded tree — 493 ft

Tallest living tree — 366 ft

Statue of Liberty — 301 ft

Tallest Christmas tree — 221 ft

Tallest sunflower — 25 ft
Tallest person — 8.9 ft

NOW TRY THESE MIGHTY GIANTS FOR SIZE!

BLOOMING
Huge!

Growing bigger can mean the difference between life and death in the amazing plant kingdom.

In tropical rain forests, if trees don't reach up to other tree tops, they won't get enough light to live. And because of the thickness of the trees, plants on the forest floor have to grow huge leaves to capture all the available light they can to survive.

A plant called an aroid in Borneo has the biggest leaves in the world- up to 9 feet long and 6 feet wide. This enables it to soak up the merest hint of light. And the longest leaves in the world belong to the raffia palm, at up to 65 feet long – that's bigger than most trees!

▼ *Witnessing the spectacular opening of a giant rafflesia flower*

DYING TO BLOOM!

Sometimes, though, plants appear to be big for no reason. And the plant with the world's biggest flower is one of those. Called the rafflesia, it lives on vines in rain forests in South-east Asia. Starting as a lump on the vine, the rafflesia spends weeks getting larger and larger until it suddenly blooms into a huge five-petaled flower. It can measure over 3 feet in diameter.

Locals say it smells of rotting flesh and call it the "corpse flower." Luckily, flies love the strange fragrance, which is just as well as they have the job of pollinating it. However, the

IN AT THE DEEP END

The deepest roots ever discovered belonged to a wild fig tree in South Africa. They went 394 feet into the earth.

busy buzzers have got to be quick – the world's largest flower only lives for four days before it rots and becomes a corpse itself! Phew!

LONG SHOT

The plant with the longest stem in the world is the rattan, a climbing palm of Southeast Asia.

◀ *Huge buttress roots support mighty rain forest trees.*

◀ *Rattan stems grow until they find a suitable tree to hook onto.*

Its stem is covered in sharp tendrils with hooks on the end. The tendrils snag onto a tree, which it then uses to help it climb up to the tree-tops. Sometimes the tree is not strong enough to support it and the rattan falls to the forest floor with the tree. But it doesn't give up.

The rattan grows rapidly along the ground looking for another tree to grab onto. When this happens, the stems can stretch more than 500 feet – the same size as the tallest tree ever recorded. That's what you call determination!

MONSTER MUNCH

Bernard Lavery from Llanharry, Wales, is the world champ when it comes to growing giant vegetables. He holds 15 world records for growing the biggest and best – from the most massive vegetable marrow at 108 lbs, to the chunkiest cabbage of 124 lbs! Bernard reckons they taste just as good as normal veggies, just a bit more of a mouthful!

What the insect hasn't spotted, though, are the tiny trigger hairs on the inside of each leaf.

If the insect touches these hairs, the leaves snap shut, trapping it in a leafy prison. The trigger hairs have to be touched at least twice so the flytrap can be sure it really is an insect resting on it and not just a falling leaf. Once happy with its trapped prey, the cunning carnivore produces digestive juices that dissolve the insect, providing it with a six-legged snack. Yum! And 24 hours later, the flytrap is ready for its next meal.

▲ The sundew plant senses lunch has arrived.

PITCHER THIS!

Another type of plant that eats insects to make up for missing nutrients is the pitcher plant. Both the Venus's-flytrap and the pitcher plant are found in small areas of North and South America, but pitchers are most common in Southeast Asia.

These clever carnivores entice insects into their pitcher, or pot-shaped, leaves with the promise of sweet nectar. As the insect moves around the pitcher, its feet become clogged in a waxy substance produced by the leaf. Or it can lose its

The biggest pitcher plant, which plummets to a depth of 12 inches, holds over 4 pints of liquid. It can trap an awful lot of flies – and even mice!

In places like marshes and bogs, where essential nutrients are washed away, plants turn to another source of food – insects.

The most famous of these carnivores is the Venus's-flytrap. These preying plants look harmless enough, but insects soon find out how dangerous they really are.

The munching marvels have two leaves that are joined along one side and lie invitingly open, encouraging any passing insect to come and try the tasty nectar.

SNAP HAPPY!

Meet the meat-munching plants

footing on slippery downward-pointing hairs. Either way, the insect soon tumbles into a pool of water at the bottom of the pitcher. As it struggles to escape, the plant releases a digestive acid so strong that the insect will become a hollow shell within hours.

Some cunning frogs know that flies can't resist the smell of pitcher plants, so they lie in wait inside the plant until a foolish fly comes along. The frogs have to be careful, though, because if they slip into the pool at the bottom, they, too, will become part of the pitcher's pantry. Gulp!

MORE STICKY SITUATIONS

Sundew plants grow in marshes all over the world and get their name from the glistening droplets on their leaves.

Unfortunately for inquisitive insects, it's not dew, but glue!

If an insect, such as a fly, lands on the glue and becomes stuck, the leaf folds around to enclose the foolish fly before producing special digestive juices to break it down.

Much smaller insects, such as mosquito larvae, are the bladderwort's prey. Living in water, the bladderwort has tiny, transparent pockets, with doors that swing open when they're touched by a small insect. The insect then gets sucked in before the door quickly slams shut, and the bladderwort settles down to its meal. Two hours later its trap is reset, ready for its next victim.

MISERLY MISTLETOE

In Western Australia, most plants don't flower during the very hot summer. However, one tree chooses just this time of year to blossom and is known as the Christmas tree.

It thrives in searing heat because it steals water and nutrients from all of the plants around it. When one of its roots meets another plant's roots, this member of the mistletoe family cuts the other root in half before selfishly sucking up its goodness.

However, even mistletoe isn't safe. There are some varieties that only live on other mistletoe! Bah, humbug!

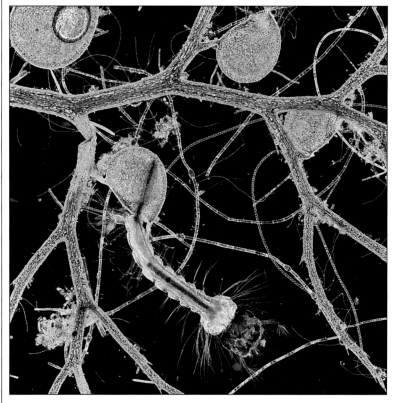

▲ **Mosquito larvae are the hungry bladderwort's prey.**

They're armed and dangerous!

IT'S

▲ *If the threatening spikes don't keep animals at bay, the buffalo acacia has a second trick to defend itself.*

Plants are always in danger of being eaten, so they've developed impressive ways of protecting themselves.

CHEMICAL WARFARE

The leaves of buffalo acacia trees from east Africa are surrounded by very sharp thorns. But even that doesn't stop nimble-tongued animals with tough mouths from having a nibble, so the plant has developed a second line of defense.

After an animal has been eating it for a short time, the plant produces a disgusting-tasting chemical in its leaves. What's more, it also gives off a nasty gas to warn any acacias within 150 feet that there are enemy animals in the area. This triggers the other acacias to start producing the bad chemical, too.

By the time the animal has been put off by the yucky leaves on the first tree and moved on to the next, the leaves of the second tree are primed for action!

◀ *Spiky spines on trunk of palm tree from Singapore*

WAR!

▲ ANT PATROL

The bull's horn acacia protects itself with its own private police force. Armies of ants living inside the tree's thorns patrol the tree and bite intruding animal visitors until they go away.

They also bite through any plants or seedlings growing near their tree that threaten the acacia's space. In return, the tree produces fatty growths and sweet nectar for the ants to eat, as well as giving them their own home sweet home!

Ants also have a special relationship with the hydnophytum plant (also called the ant plant) that grows on mangrove trees in the tropics. The hydnophytum has a swollen stem the size of a football, which is protected by sharp prickles on the outside and an intricate network of tunnels inside.

Some tunnels have smooth walls and some are rough. Ants live in the smooth-walled tunnels and leave insect remains and other waste in the rough-walled tunnels. The plant then extracts nutrients from the ants' garbage dump. Clever stuff!

STUCK ON YOU

The rubber tree has its own sticky solution to naughty nibblers. If a predator takes a bite of a rubber tree, it produces a substance that acts like a very strong glue. Before the predator even has time to swallow, its mouth is all gummed up!

▲ *The hospitable multichambered ant plant*

▲ YOU'RE NUTS!

Many trees wrap their seeds in a hard shell to protect them from hungry animals. Brazil-nut shells are very tough, and most animals can't break them – apart from a determined rodent called an agouti.

With its strong teeth, the agouti can open a bertholletia tree's fruit, which contains up to 20 Brazil nuts. As that's often more than the agouti needs, it buries the rest in different places for later. Luckily, the agouti tends to be rather forgetful and can't always remember where it's stashed its secret store. So the seeds are left to grow in peace in just the right amount of earth. The agouti ends up doing the plant a favor!

SHARP SHOCK

When an insect lands on one of the mimosa tree's tasty-looking leaves, the tree suddenly folds up the leaf tightly onto its stem. And if the pesky insect persists in trying to chomp away, the tree then lowers the leaf to reveal nasty sharp spikes on its stalk. Because of these dramatic defenses, the mimosa is one of the most common trees in the tropics.

DANGER!

Plant poisons are a deadly serious matter!

▲ *It might look pretty, but this hemlock's a killer.*

Plants have developed many powerful poisons to ward off animals and insects. Some, like bracken, contain enough cyanide poison in their leaves to blind any animal that eats them. Others, like the oleander, are so deadly that a single leaf will kill by causing a heart attack.

Many poisonous plants are close relations of common foods. Two of the most dangerous, water hemlock and spotted hemlock, belong to the same family as carrots and parsley. And the well-named deadly nightshade is a relative of the potato. In fact, potatoes that have been exposed to the light and turned green contain a very potent poison. Beware!

TOADSTOOL TERROR!

Wild toadstools and mushrooms have a reputation for being very poisonous. But even though most of them are actually harmless, fungi such as the death cap, the sickener, and the destroying angel all deserve their stomach-churning names. In fact, just one small death cap mushroom will kill an adult, and this mushroom is responsible for nine out of ten deaths caused by fungi.

▶ KILL OR CURE?

The most deadly of all plant poisons, though, is curare. It's made by South American Indians from two different rain forest plants. The actual ingredients are a closely guarded secret, but once perfected, the curare is smeared on the tips of blow-darts. When an animal is hit by a dart, the curare enters the body and kills the animal – immediately.

Even though they usually have the opposite effect, some poisonous plants are used by doctors to help cure patients. For example, curare is used during surgical operations to relax muscles. And the life-threatening poison found in purple fox-glove (right) is used to help people with heart disorders.

▲ *These deadly seeds are used to poison arrows.*

way of keeping competing plants at a distance. It gives off a poison through its roots, so that anything that comes too near dies. This ensures that the creosote plant soaks up all of the available water for itself.

▼ DEADLY BEAUTY SECRETS

Deadly nightshade is also known as *belladonna*, the Latin name for "beautiful lady." A few centuries ago women put extracts of this poisonous plant into their eyes. It would make their pupils appear bigger and the women seem more attractive – hence the name *belladonna*. Even today, extracts of this substance are sometimes used in eye surgery to expand pupils.

▲ KEEP YOUR DISTANCE

The creosote bush that grows in North American deserts has found a cunning

Poisonous plants have been used throughout history to kill people. The first recorded poisoning is that of the ancient Greek philosopher Socrates. In 339 B.C., he was made to drink the deadly juice of spotted hemlock after being found guilty of preaching against Greek gods.

Four hundred years later, the Roman emperor Claudius was poisoned by his wife Agrippina. She wanted him dead so that her son Nero could become emperor. She told a cook to prepare his favorite dish (now known as Caesar's mushrooms). Then she squeezed the juice of a death cap mushroom into it. Its poison doesn't show symptoms for several hours, and by the time that Claudius discovered he'd been fed the deadly ingredient it was too late.

▲ *Gulp! Socrates is forced to drink deadly hemlock.*

▲ *This hand-picked cotton could end up in your band uniform!*

fibers. Then these fibers are separated and cleaned before being spun into useful cotton thread.

Some plants also make good alternatives to traditional building materials. Long, thin rattans from the tropics can be used to make furniture, baskets, and ropes. They're even used to tie wood together instead of hammering in nails.

TREE TAPS

If you've got a sweet tooth, perhaps you should seek out a North American sugar-maple tree.

This tree yields delicious maple syrup, which is extracted by putting a spout into a drilled hole in the tree. The sap then runs out and can be boiled down until just the sweet syrup remains. One

▲ *Collecting maple syrup – fresh from the trees*

From furniture and **clothing to medicine and food, plants and trees are vital to our daily life.** Apart from a whole harvest of delicious fruits and vegetables that we've grown to love, trees and plants produce all sorts of other useful raw materials.

Cotton, for instance, comes from a sub-tropical plant that is now grown from China and Russia to the Sudan and Brazil. The cotton is harvested when the cotton plant's seed pods burst open to reveal a mass of white

RICH PICKINGS

tree can produce 30 gallons of sap a year – but it can take around 13 gallons of sap to make just 2 pints of maple syrup.

Maya Indians from Central America have been making use of the rubber tree's juices since the 11th century. Nowadays, most rubber is produced on plantations in Indonesia, Sri Lanka, and Malaysia. And although synthetic alternatives have been perfected, real rubber is still the favorite when it comes to tires for cars, trucks, and airplanes.

▲ VALUABLE SPICES

Flowers, leaves, and the barks of plants have always been valued for the way they can preserve and improve the flavor of food. In the Middle Ages they were valued so highly that pepper was actually used as money!

But that's nothing compared with the price tag on the golden spice saffron : ounce for ounce it costs more than gold! It comes from a certain type of crocus, and over 150 flowers are needed to make just a gram of the precious spice. So you can be sure that the recipes that contain saffron are very rich indeed!

CLASSIC CURES

For many centuries plants have been used as medicinal remedies. One of the world's most common drugs, aspirin, originally came from the bark of the willow tree. Meanwhile, quinine, a drug that comes from the bark of the cinchona tree, has saved millions of people from being killed by malaria.

Some people believe that plants can be used with the body's own healing powers to keep us well. This practice is known as homeopathy and uses minute extracts of plants to reproduce the symptoms of a disease. As a result, the body's own healing processes are said to be boosted and strengthened.

Extracts of a certain type of periwinkle are being used to treat children suffering from leukemia, and many synthetic medicines are based on traditional plant cures. Even with today's sophisticated medicinal technology, a quarter of modern medicines contain one or more plant extracts.

The copaiba langsdorfii tree of Central America produces a sap that is so similar to diesel fuel it can be poured straight into the fuel tank!

▲ *Tapping rubber from a tree in Thailand*

▲ *Periwinkles could be the key to a cure for cancer.*

FABULOUS FUNGUS

The world wouldn't be the same place without fungi!

Fungi aren't really plants. They have no roots, stems, or leaves, but these groovy growths still fascinate botanists. They're made up of tiny, branching threads in soil, tree trunks, and other places. Most of the time we don't even know they are there – it's only when a fungus produces a toadstool or mushroom that we become aware of it.

These toadstools or, more correctly, fruiting bodies come in all shapes and sizes – from a small, slimy ear-shaped fungus to the whopping chicken of the woods fungus, which can weigh in at over 100 pounds!

▲ *The ear-shaped Auricularia Auriculajudae*

HIGH SPORES

In a similar way to a plant producing a flower, fungi grow fruiting bodies so that they can reproduce. But unlike flowers, fungi don't have seeds. Instead, they use microscopic spores that can grow without needing to be fertilized. These spores are carried by the wind or insects to their new growing place. Often the spores fail, so a mushroom will release up to 10,000 million spores in a few days to ensure its survival.

Fungi play a vital role in the plant world by breaking down dead leaves, wood, and other matter into nutrients that plants can use. Without fungi, the world would be littered with dead leaves, trees, and other plants.

In fact, fungi often help old trees to survive. They help dead wood to rot and slowly hollow out the insides of the tree trunk. This actually makes the tree more resistant to strong winds than before.

FUNGAL FOOD ▶

The largest edible fungus is the giant puffball. It can grow to over 9 feet in circumference and, like all members of the puffball family, gets rid of its spores by "puffing" them out at the slightest touch. Even a raindrop on its brittle shell can spark off the

▲ *Sniffing out truffles in the French countryside*

powerful puffing.

But as obvious as the puffball is, some edible mushrooms can only be found by animals. The highly prized truffle grows underground and gives off the scent of a male pig. Female pigs can be used to root them out, though more often special dogs called truffle hounds are used. It's well worth the effort, because once found, truffles are worth a lot of money, as they're considered a very extravagant delicacy!

FIRM FUNGAL FRIENDS

Some plants simply couldn't survive without the help of fungi – many orchid seeds need

Fungi are made of chitin, the same material as insect skeletons and horns and claws of mammals.

▲ *The mysterious disappearing ghost orchid*

▲ *The eggs-quisite bird's-nest fungus*

HUMONGOUS FUNGUS

When it comes to titanic toadstools, the honey or boot-lace fungus beats them all. A single plant in a forest in Washington state is believed to be up to 1,000 years old! It's grown so large it now sprawls over 1,400 acres!
And it's still growing!

certain fungi around them in order for them to germinate. The rare ghost orchid, which grows in very dark, damp woods, actually lives off a fungus that feeds on rotting leaves. It has no leaves or true roots of its own and relies entirely on the fungus for all its food. In fact, there is nothing aboveground to indicate that it is there at all. For that reason, the ghost orchid has been declared extinct several times, only for its stalk to suddenly appear out of the ground bearing pink and yellow flowers.

▲ *The golden-colored honey fungus*

▲ *Luminous mushrooms light up tropical forest floors, attracting animal messengers.*

HOLD YOUR NOSE!

Insects and animals are attracted to plants by smells, but often the attraction isn't attractive at all! Most plants produce their seeds by fertilizing female parts of the plant with the male pollen from another plant. To get that pollen from plant to plant, flying insects are often employed as pollen deliverers.

To persuade the insects to visit the plant, many offer nectar, a sweet food, as well as letting off an irresistible perfume. They may be irresistible to animals, but humans will certainly turn their noses up at some of the "tempting" fragrances, such as the aptly named dead horse arum and rancid-smelling stapelia flower.

BATTY ABOUT FRUIT

Wild bananas and certain cacti use a different type of winged messenger: bats. They are drawn by heady perfumes and can be found burying their heads in flowers, looking for nectar. Fruits like peaches and figs have a fragrance that tempts animals to eat them. When they munch away, the animals also swallow seeds that are later dispersed in their droppings. Some, like the durian fruit of Southeast Asia, can be smelled half a mile away! This awesome odor is often compared to

Not all flowers come up smelling like roses!

Napoleon loved perfume and used to pour eau de Cologne all over his head and shoulders, using up to 60 bottles. Eau la la!

▲ *Durian perfume? No thanks!*

the smell of sewers or rotten fish, but the flesh inside is said to be odor-free and delicious. Local people, orangutans, and even tigers can often be found feasting on this foul-smelling fruit!

HEAVEN SCENT

For thousands of years, people have made perfumes from plants and flowers, and traditionally they are very expensive. In the Bible, the three wise men brought baby Jesus valuable gold and two expensive fragrant gifts of frankincense and myrrh, and these biblical fragrances are still used in perfume manufacture today.

Perfumes are made of up to 100 ingredients, often including jasmine, lavender (left), and rose (below). But one of the most expensive scents comes from the oil of the bergamot tree, a type of bitter orange grown in southern Italy.

BEE SERIOUS!

Male euglossina bees in Brazil splash on perfume to attract females. They collect a fragrant oil from orchids in spongy receptacles on their hind legs. Then they release the smell into the air by beating their wings over their perfume-soaked legs. Fan-tastic!

This tiny tree (right) has reached its full height at just 8 inches tall and won't grow another inch higher in its 100-year life.

The practice of cultivating dwarf trees began over 1,000 years ago in China, but it was the Japanese who turned it into an art form known as bonsai (or tray planting).

The pint-sized plants are miniature versions of full-sized trees that live in the wild. In order for them to grow correctly, branches are regularly pruned and then made to grow into the desired shape by twisting them around pieces of wire. Then the roots are cut back so that the plant can remain in a small container.

These tree-mendous masterpieces follow the seasons in the same way as normal trees, producing flowers in spring and dropping leaves in autumn – even though the flowers and leaves are much smaller than normal. They can also live for hundreds of years – the oldest known bonsai tree is over 600 years old and is said to be priceless. It's still growing strong today!

> Epiphytic orchids living in the rainforest canopy produce the smallest-known seeds. They are so tiny, 992.25 million of them would weigh just one gram.

POCKET-SIZED PRICKER

Cacti come in all shapes and sizes, but the tiniest of all these sharp-spined plants is the Blossfeldia liliputana. This Argentinian mini marvel has heads that measure a minuscule 3/8 inch across while its delicate white flowers grow to just 1/4 inch wide.

WATER WONDER

The world's smallest plant is a duckweed that grows in ponds in Australia (magnified right). It is only 0.024 in. long and weighs about 1/100,000 oz. It's so tiny that you could fit 35 of them across one fingernail! The fruit that it produces weighs a feather-weight 1/400,000 oz. and looks like a fig – although you need a microscope just to see it.

Small is beautiful
TEENY gREENIES

◄ *Whopping water lilies can grow up to 8 feet wide!*

▼ *Mangroves prepare for the swell of the tide, pushing their spear-shaped seeds into the mud.*

Plants living in ponds, lakes, and rivers don't have to worry about getting enough water to drink – it's all around them. But they still need to make sure they get enough light.

The giant water lily that grows in the Amazon jungle ensures that it gets all the light it needs by having huge circular leaves. These huge leaves can grow up to 8 feet across and are so strong that a child can sit on one without fear of sinking. Unbe-leaf-able!

At places where rivers meet the sea, plants have to cope with the constant change between freshwater and salty seawater. Mangrove swamps in tropical countries have found a clever way of getting rid of the extra salt they absorb – they concentrate salt in their sap

SOARING SEAWEED ►
The Pacific giant kelp grows up to 200 feet tall and shoots up from the seabed at a rate of 18 inches a day. There's nothing weedy about that!

WATER WONDERS

and move it into leaves that are about to die. That way, when the leaf falls off, it takes the unwanted salt with it.

Plants in the swamp also have to face swirling tides stirring up the mud they're trying to set their seeds in. One tree gets around this by having long, spear-shaped seeds that drop off the tree, falling straight into the mud. As soon as the seed lands it grows tiny roots to prepare itself for the swell of the incoming tide.

And should a seed be washed out to sea, it will float happily along for months until it comes in contact with fresh water again. Then it will start floating vertically, ready for the moment when it gets stuck in the mud, ready for rooting.

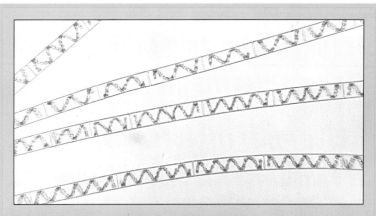

SMALL WONDER

Simple, microscopic algae are the basis of all ocean life. These huge, floating, cloudlike groups are eaten by tiny fish and other animals, which in turn are eaten by bigger fish, and so on. So in the end, all ocean life is dependent on the tiny algae.

However, it's not just ocean life that needs algae — we do, too. It's the most important factor for maintaining oxygen levels in the atmosphere. So breathe a sigh of relief — we wouldn't be here without those tiny algae.

LIVING IN HARMONY

Corals may look like plants, but they are actually animals. Sometimes you can see the tiny sea anemone-like creatures coming out of coral reefs and waving their tentacles. These tiny creatures are known as polyps and contain minute organisms within them called algae.

The algae provide the polyps with food, while the polyps' waste products give the algae their essential nutrients. What's even more clever is that the coral polyp builds a coral reef shelter for them both out of limestone. Good reef!

NOW THAT'S *Clever!*

Nifty tricks from the plant kingdom

▲ *Epiphytic lichens set up house on a juniper tree.*

Plants have developed all sorts of clever ways to make sure they survive and thrive.

TALL PLOYS

Even though there's no shortage of rain in the rain forests, plants called epiphytes, which live in the top branches of the canopy, don't have long enough roots to soak up water from the ground. Instead, some epiphytes, such as air orchids, dangle their roots in the humid air to absorb water. Alternatively, they spread roots over branches and leaves to suck up any droplets trickling by.

Other types of epiphytes called bromeliads form bucketlike structures that can hold over 10 quarts of water. These are very handy for monkeys who drink from them, plus tree frogs and other mini-creatures who use bromeliads as treetop ponds. As well as water, bromeliads collect dead insects, rotting leaves, and animal droppings, and these provide a great menu of nutrients for the plant.

▼ *Pitcher plants are handy ponds for hungry tree frogs.*

▶ CREEPING KILLER

Most epiphytes don't harm the tree that they live in, but the strangler fig is a murderer. This epiphyte grows slowly down the canopy, encircling a tree trunk with its creepers until it reaches the ground. Once there, the strangler fig starts to take up nutrients and water from the soil, prompting it to start growing very vigorously.

Before long, the whole tree has been encased in a mesh of strangler fig branches, often more than one plant. And as the lattice of the strangler fig grows, it begins to steal all the water and nutrients in the ground that were destined for the tree, then shields the tree's leaves from light with its own leaves. The tree soon dies and rots, leaving a hollow lattice of strangler fig standing on its own like an empty tower. Creepy!

BRIGHT SPARKS

Forest fires raging in hot, dry countries like Australia and Africa can cause devastation, but they are the start of new life, too. Some trees, like the huge Australian mountain ash, actually need a forest fire to be able to spread seed. When a fire sweeps though a forest, it usually burns plants on the forest floor; however, the heat from the fire causes

▲ *Australian banksia bushes rely on forest fires for their survival.*

seeds in the mountain ash's branches to crack open and fall to the ground. And whereas most plants have been burned to a crisp, this tree's seeds soon grow into a new generation of beautiful mountain ash trees.

Australian banksia bushes also need fire to reproduce. The tough seed cones won't release their contents unless they have been burned by intense heat. But once released, the seeds flourish without competition in freshly fertilized ground.

READY, AIM, FIRE!

Some plants don't use insects, animals, or the wind to disperse their seeds – they just take aim and fire!
● The squirting cucumber does this by slowly filling a seed pod with liquid until it

Coconuts floating in the sea can travel massive distances from their parent tree before reaching land and germinating. Let's hope they're not shy when they get there!

is under such pressure that the pod bursts off the stalk. It catapults itself up to 20 feet away, leaving a trail of seeds on the earth, ready to grow.
● The Australian pine mistletoe uses a similar method, propelling its tiny seeds 50 feet at a speedy 30 mph.
● The broom shrub doesn't use liquid, but instead relies on its seed pod drying out. As the covers of the pod dry, they build up such tension that the two sides burst open, flinging seeds in all directions.
● But the prize for the loudest launch goes to the hura tree of Brazil. Like the broom, it flings its seeds out, but with such a resounding shot that it can be heard throughout the forest.

COPY CATS

Is it an insect? Is it a leaf?

▲ *Can you spot the leaflike praying mantis?*

Plants and animals try all sorts of disguises to fool each other.

UNBE-LEAF-ABLE!

Some insects have decided the best way to avoid being eaten is to pretend to be a part of a plant. The masters of disguise in the insect world are katydids that live in the U.S. and countries such as Costa Rica and Brazil. Long-horned grasshoppers also look incredibly like the leaves that they feed on, which means they can munch to their hearts' content without ending up as lunch themselves!

Moths make great mimics, too (see below), and this stick insect (right) is so convincing he should definitely stick to it!

▲ PLANT POSER

The stinging nettle gives anything that tries to munch it a nasty sting, so most animals stay away. The harmless deadnettle and the yellow archangel have cunningly copied its leaves, causing animals to avoid them because they believe they, too, are stingers.

BUTTERFLY BAFFLER

The passion flower vine is a favorite nibble of South America's heliconius caterpillars. So, to discourage them, the passion flower vine grows egglike knobs. Butterflies believe they are another butterfly's eggs and flit off to another plant where their caterpillars will have less competition for food. That's what you call an egg-cellent disguise!

◀ REFLECT ON THIS

The mirror orchid's flowers look and smell like a female bee, so when a male bee sees a mirror orchid flower, it tries to mate with it! As a result the orchid can push pollen onto the bee's head. And when the bee falls for the trick again on another orchid, the pollen is transferred, completing fertilization. Disguise the limit!

CROAKING LEAVES!

Frogs are a favorite food for certain animals, so to stop being eaten, some tree frogs pretend to be a leaf. If they are ever noticed they can always hop it!

▼ STONE ME!

The pebble plant found in African deserts has two stumpy leaves that look just like pebbles — so animals hardly ever notice it!

PLAYING DEAD

This South American leaf fish uses its clever disguise to sneak up on its prey by pretending it is a dead leaf floating in the water. It's got a big appetite, too, consuming its own weight in food every day.

INDEX